BLAZERS®

Extinct Monsters

Sabertooth Cat

by Janet Riehecky

Reading Consultant:
Barbara J. Fox
Reading Specialist
North Carolina State University

Content Consultant:
Professor Timothy H. Heaton
Chair of Earth Science/Physics
University of South Dakota, Vermillion

Capstone
press®

Mankato, Minnesota

Blazers is published by Capstone Press,
151 Good Counsel Drive, P.O. Box 669, Mankato, Minnesota 56002.
www.capstonepress.com

Library of Congress Cataloging-in-Publication Data
Riehecky, Janet, 1953–
    Sabertooth cat / by Janet Riehecky.
    p. cm.—(Blazers. Extinct monsters)
    Summary: "Simple text and illustrations describe sabertooth cats, how they
lived, and how they became extinct"—Provided by publisher.
    Includes bibliographical references and index.
    ISBN-13: 978-1-4296-0117-7 (hardcover)
    ISBN-10: 1-4296-0117-5 (hardcover)
    1. Smilodon fatalis—North America—Juvenile literature. 2. Smilodon
fatalis—South America—Juvenile literature. 3. Paleontology—Pleistocene—
Juvenile literature. 4. Paleontology—North America—Juvenile literature. 5.
Paleontology—South America—Juvenile literature. I. Title. II. Series.
QE882.C15R55 2008
569'.75—dc22   2006038524

Editorial Credits

Jenny Marks, editor; Ted Williams, designer; Jon Hughes and
    Russell Gooday/www.pixelshack.com, illustrators;
    Wanda Winch, photo researcher

Photo Credits

Shutterstock/Lazar Mihai-Bogdan, cover (background)
Visuals Unlimited/David Wrobel, 29 (skeleton)

1 2 3 4 5 6 12 11 10 09 08 07

**For Geoff, who has had his own encounter with Sabertooth,
with love from Aunt Janet.**

Table of Contents

A Frozen World

A million years ago, the world was bitterly cold. Sheets of ice called glaciers covered a third of the land.

Large, fierce animals ruled the earth. One of the most dangerous creatures was the smilodon (SMILE-uh-don), a sabertooth cat.

Monster Fact

The name smilodon
means "knife tooth."

Fur and Fangs

Sabertooth cats grew 7 feet (2.1 meters) long and almost 4 feet (1.2 meters) tall. Some cats weighed more than 800 pounds (363 kilograms).

Sabertooth cats had heavy, furry bodies and stubby tails. Powerful legs and big claws made these cats top predators.

Monster Fact

A sabertooth cat could roar like a lion.

A sabertooth's most deadly weapons were its 7-inch (18-centimeter) fangs. The cats opened their mouths wide to stab prey with their teeth.

Monster Fact

A sabertooth's fangs had a
razor-sharp back edge that
sank deep into prey.

Deadly Hunters

Sabertooth cats took shelter in the forests and grasslands south of the glaciers. Some people think the cats lived and hunted in packs.

Sabertooth cats probably hunted in silence. They hid in bushes or deep grass. A surprise attack awaited any animal that came too close.

Monster Fact

Sabertooth cats may have hunted big animals like horses and mammoths.

Sabertooths quickly leaped upon their prey. They pinned the animal down with their strong legs and sharp claws.

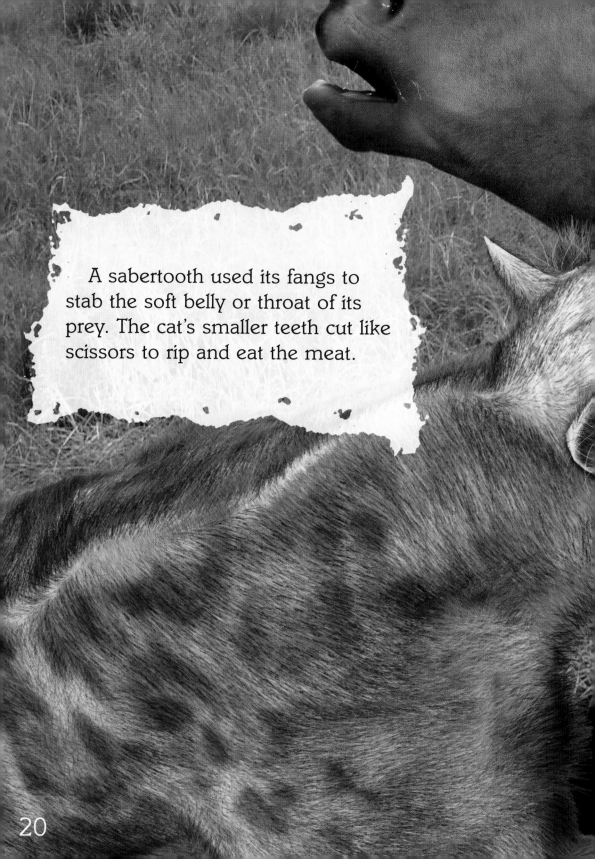

A sabertooth used its fangs to stab the soft belly or throat of its prey. The cat's smaller teeth cut like scissors to rip and eat the meat.

Sabertooth cats may have shared meat with weak members of the pack. But packs weren't always peaceful. Healthy cats probably fought for meat and mates.

23

A Monster Disappears

For at least 2 million years, the smilodon roamed North and South America. Other sabertooth cats lived all over the world.

About 10,000 years ago, sabertooth cats and many other huge creatures became extinct. The reason for their disappearance is a mystery.

In museums, you can see all that's left of the monstrous cats—fossils of bones, claws, and frightening teeth.

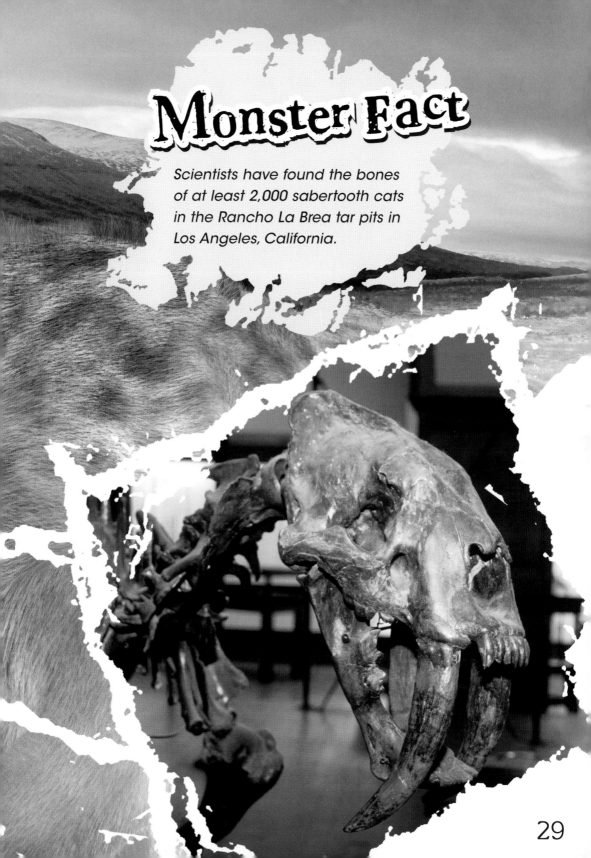

Monster Fact

Scientists have found the bones of at least 2,000 sabertooth cats in the Rancho La Brea tar pits in Los Angeles, California.

Glossary

bitter (BIT-ur)—very harsh or unpleasant

extinct (ek-STINGKT)—no longer living; an extinct animal is one that has died out, with no more of its kind.

fang (FANG)—a long, sharp, pointed tooth

fossil (FOSS-uhl)—the remains or a trace of an animal or plant that is preserved in rock or in the earth

glacier (GLAY-shur)—a large, slow-moving sheet of ice

mate (MATE)—the male or female partner in a pair of animals

monstrous (MON-struss)—large and frightening

predator (PRED-uh-tur)—an animal that hunts other animals for food

prey (PRAY)—an animal that is hunted by another animal for food

stubby (STUH-bee)—thick and short in length

Read More

Frost, Helen. *Sabertooth Cat*. Dinosaurs and Prehistoric Animals. Mankato, Minn.: Capstone Press, 2005.

Gray, Susan Heinrichs. *Saber-toothed Cats*. Exploring Dinosaurs and Prehistoric Creatures. Chanhassen, Minn.: Child's World, 2005.

Matthews, Rupert. *Sabretooth*. Gone Forever! Chicago: Heinemann, 2003.

Internet Sites

FactHound offers a safe, fun way to find Internet sites related to this book. All of the sites on FactHound have been researched by our staff.

Here's how:
1. Visit *www.facthound.com*
2. Choose your grade level.
3. Type in this book ID **1429601175** for age-appropriate sites. You may also browse subjects by clicking on letters, or by clicking on pictures and words.
4. Click on the **Fetch It** button.

FactHound will fetch the best sites for you!

Index